D1162674

How Do you Travel?
by Kathleen Joy Campion

How Do you Travel? by Kathleen Joy Campion

This is a work of fiction. All names of characters, places, and events are products of the author's imagination. Any resemblance to real persons, living or dead, is purely coincidental.

ISBN: 978-1-64934-156-3 (Paperback)
ISBN: 978-1-64934-157-0 (Hardback)

Printed in the United States of America.

Rustik Haws LLC
100 S. Ashley Drive, Suite 600
Tampa, FL 33602
https://www.rustikhaws.com/

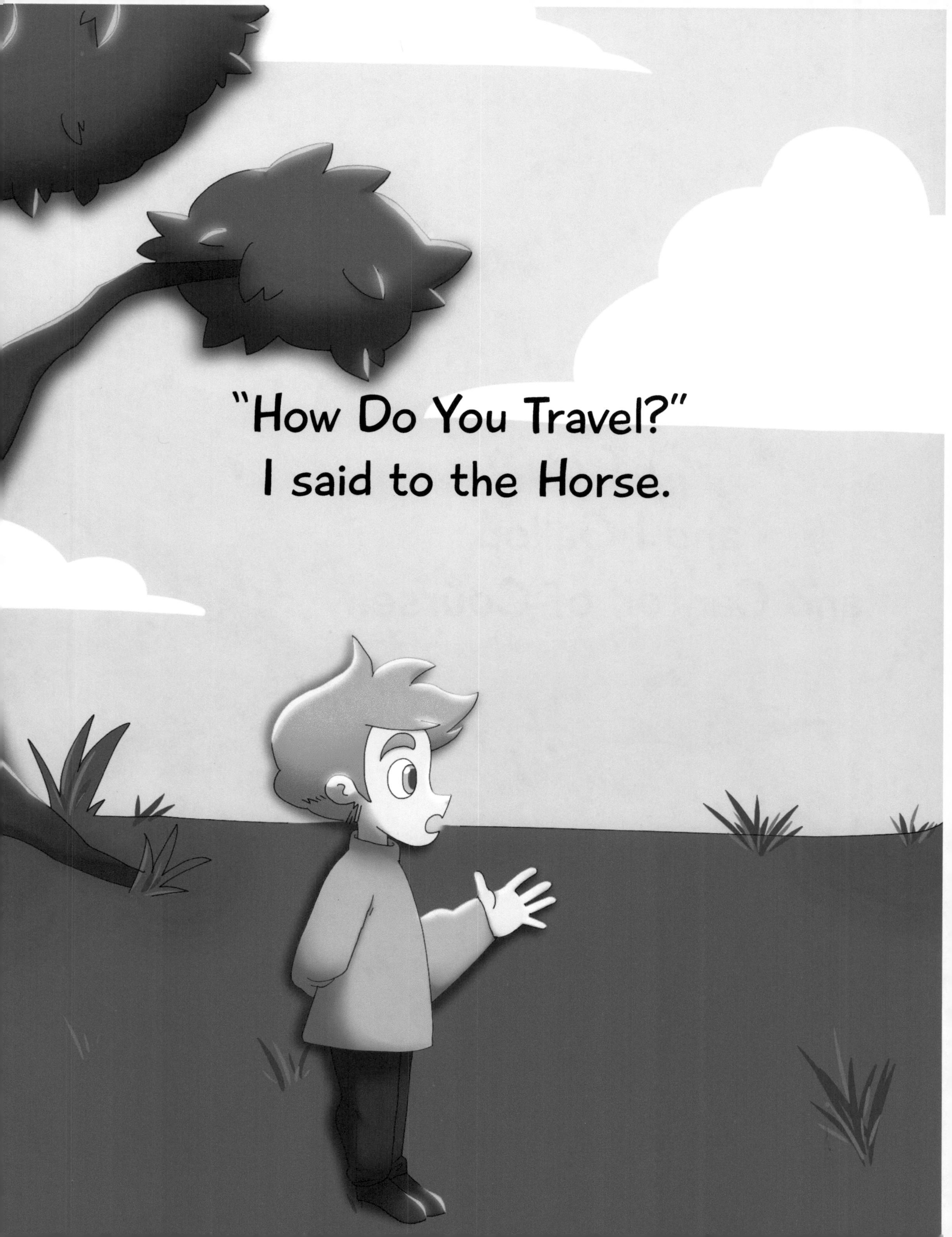

"How Do You Travel?"
I said to the Horse.

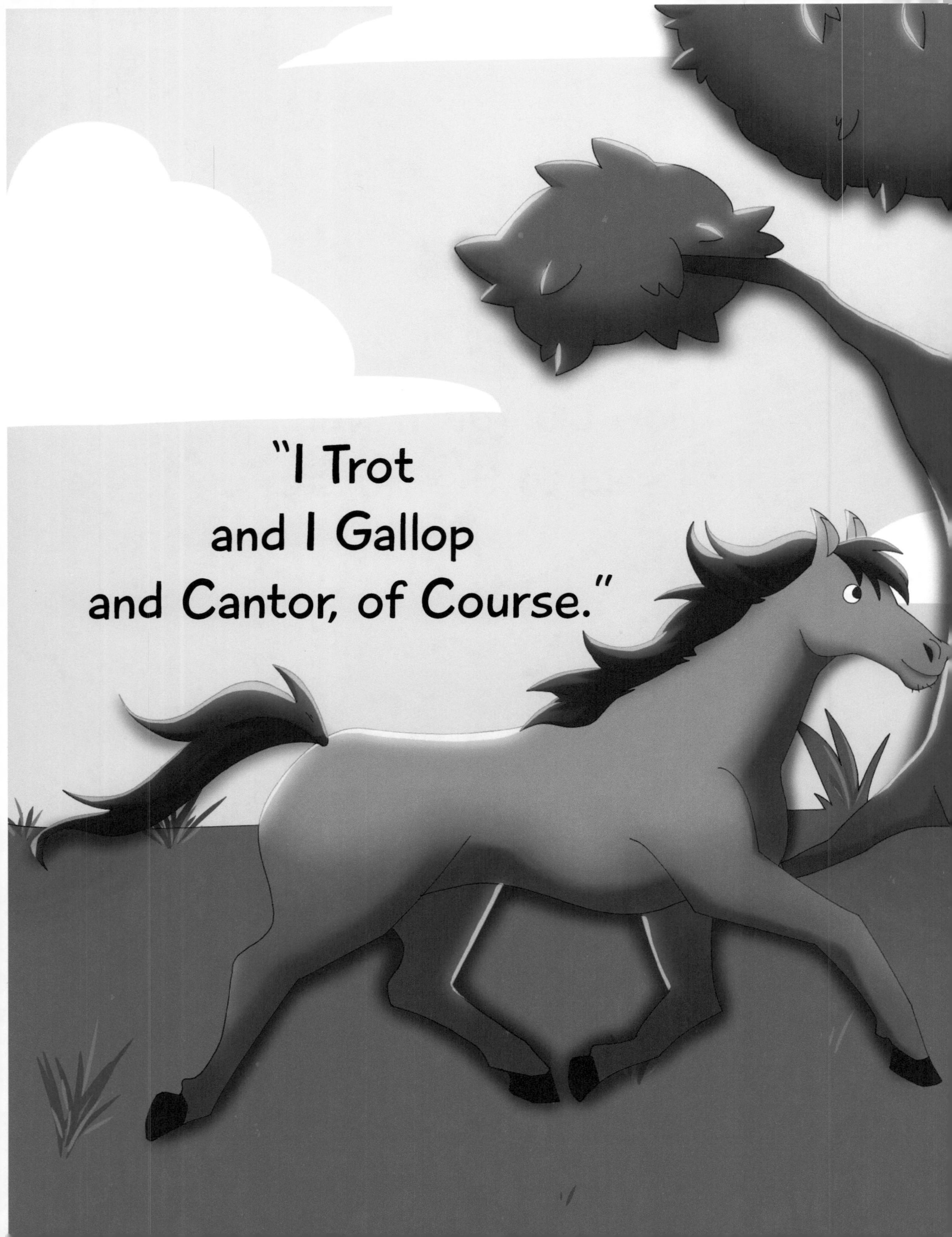

"I Trot
and I Gallop
and Cantor, of Course."

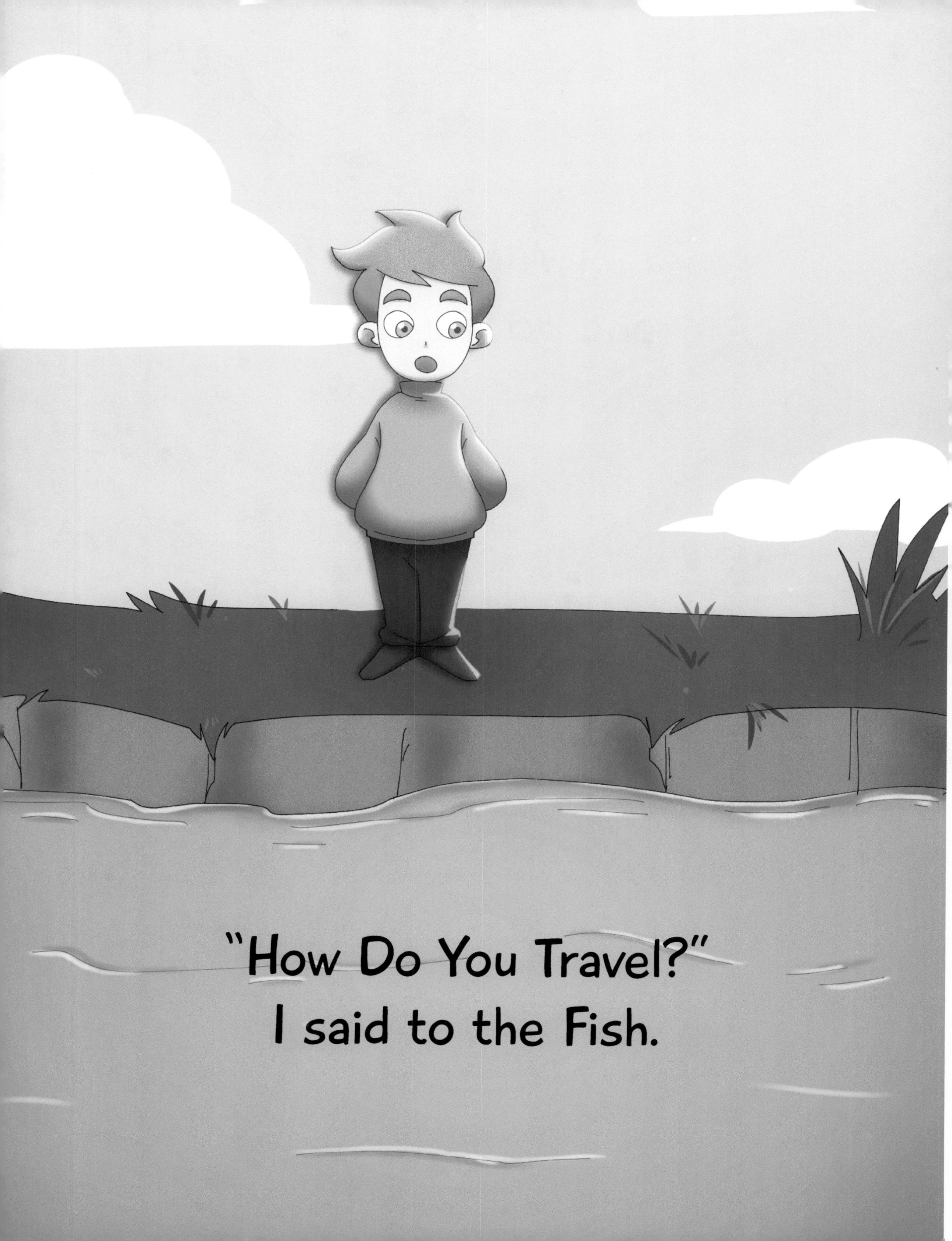

"How Do You Travel?"
I said to the Fish.

"I Wiggle my Fins
and go where I wish."

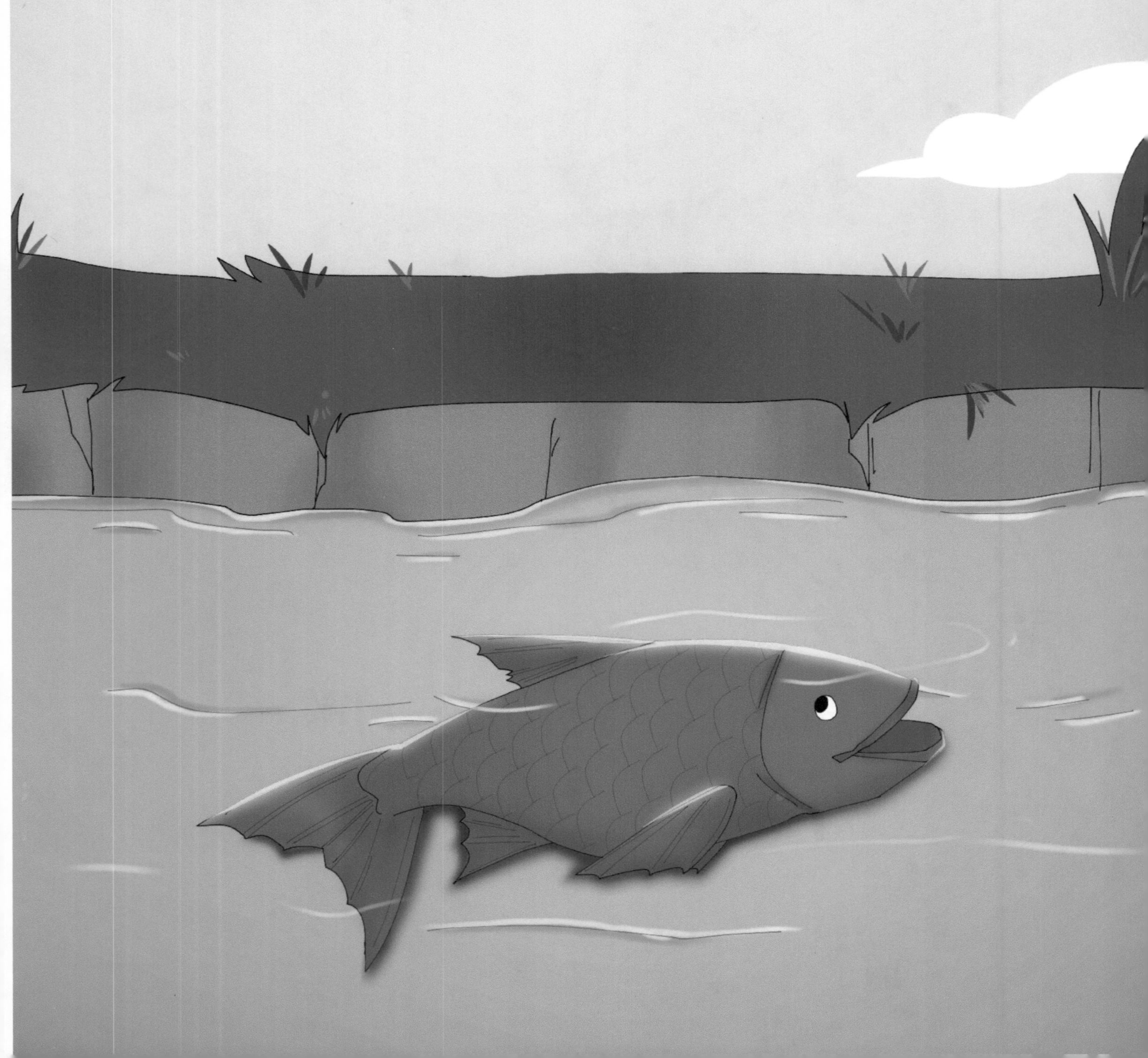

"How Do You Travel?"
I said to the Bird.

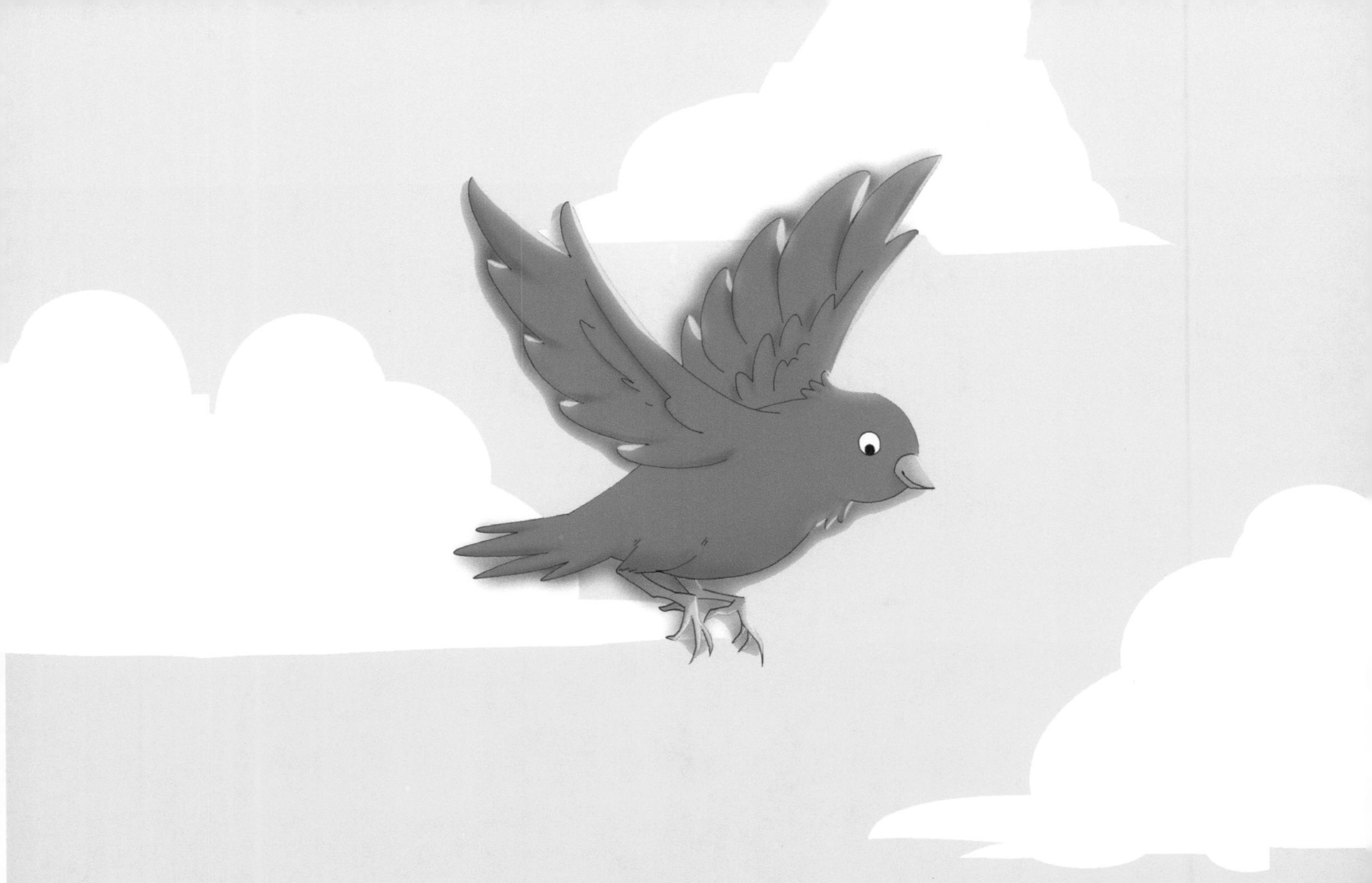

"I Just Flap my wings
anything else is absurd!"

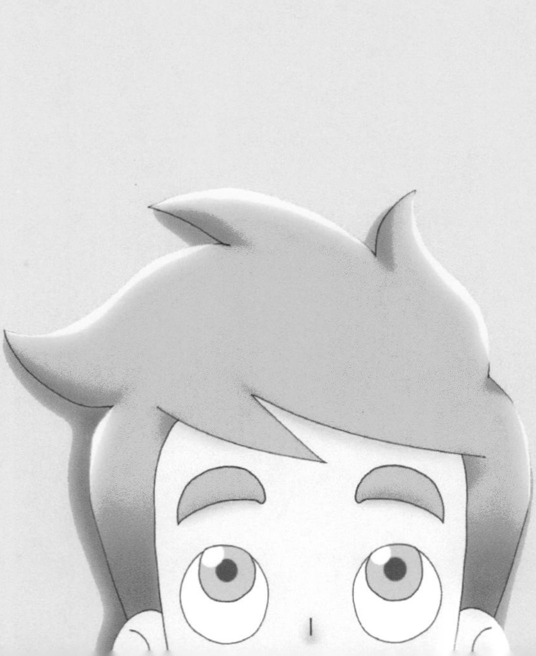

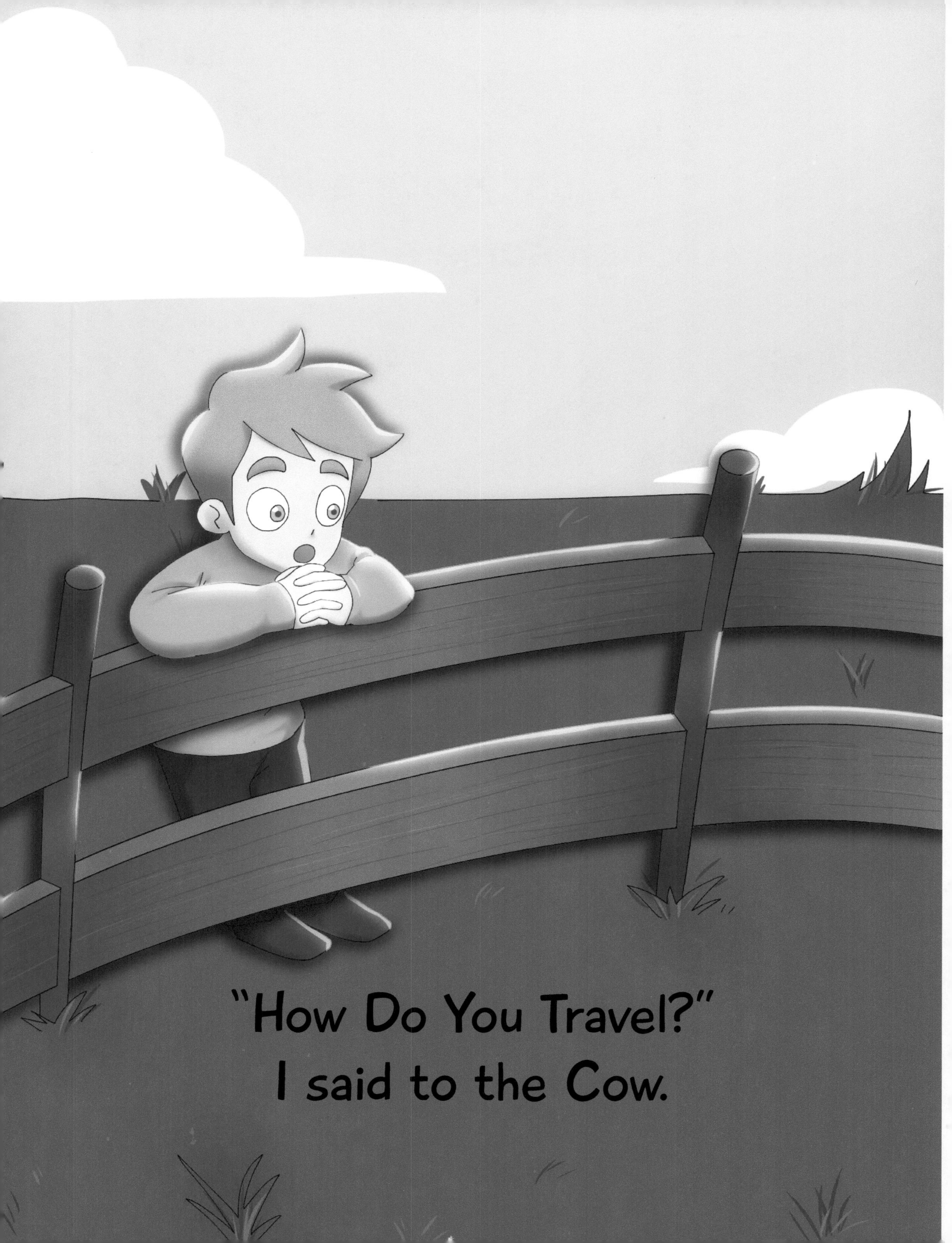

"How Do You Travel?"
I said to the Cow.

"I just move a little
though some ask me how."

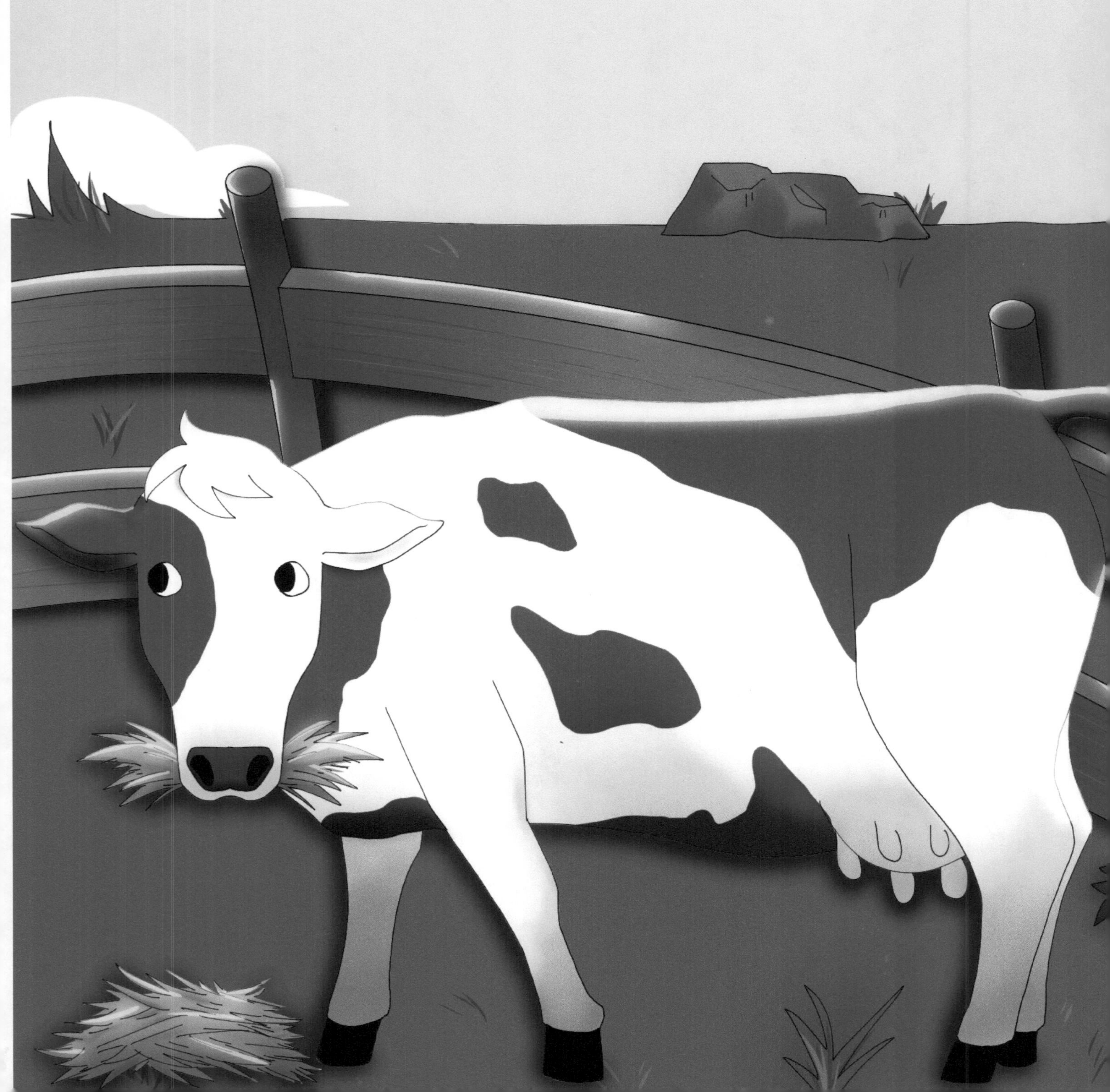

"How Do You Travel?"
I said to the Snail.

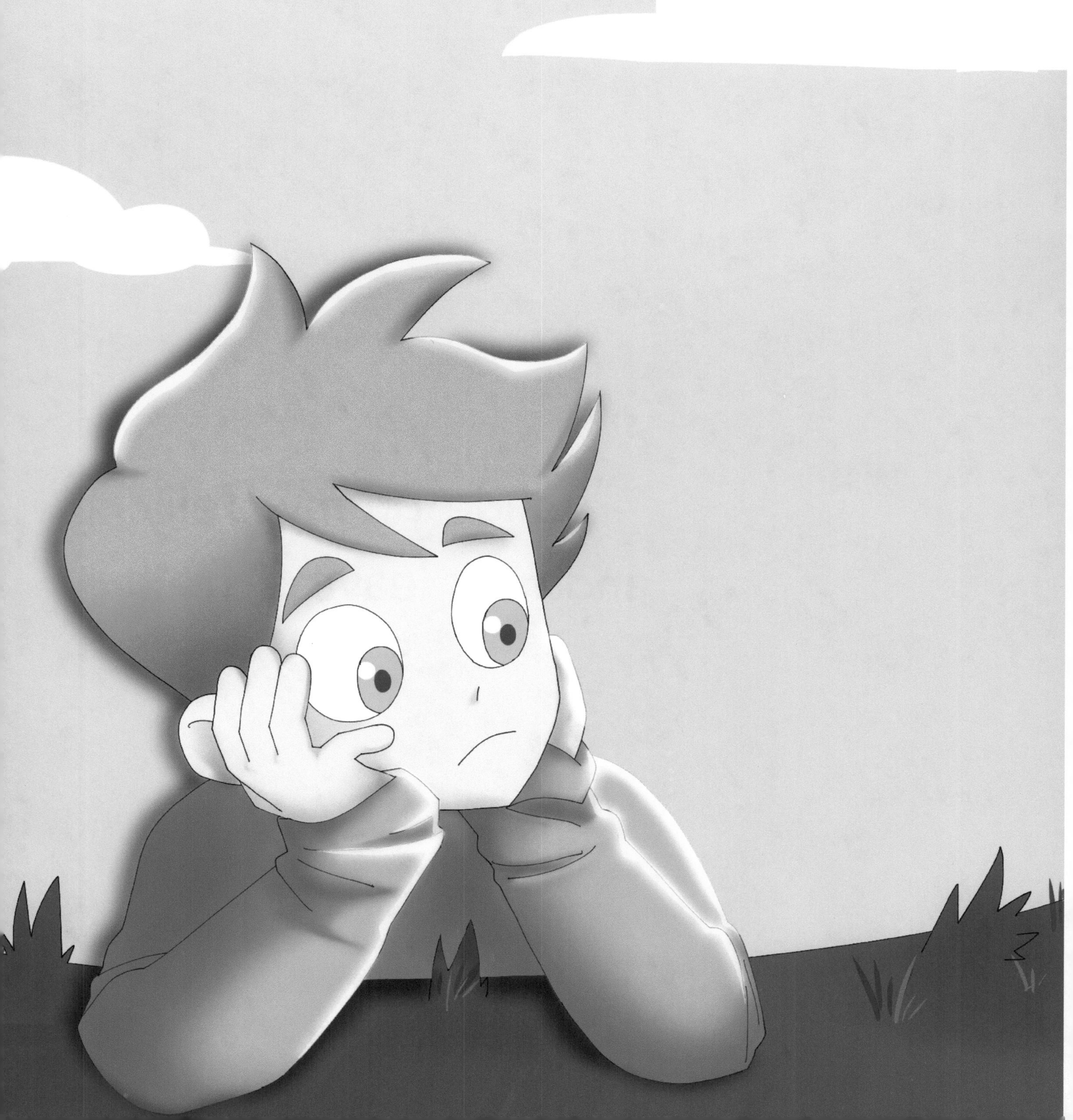

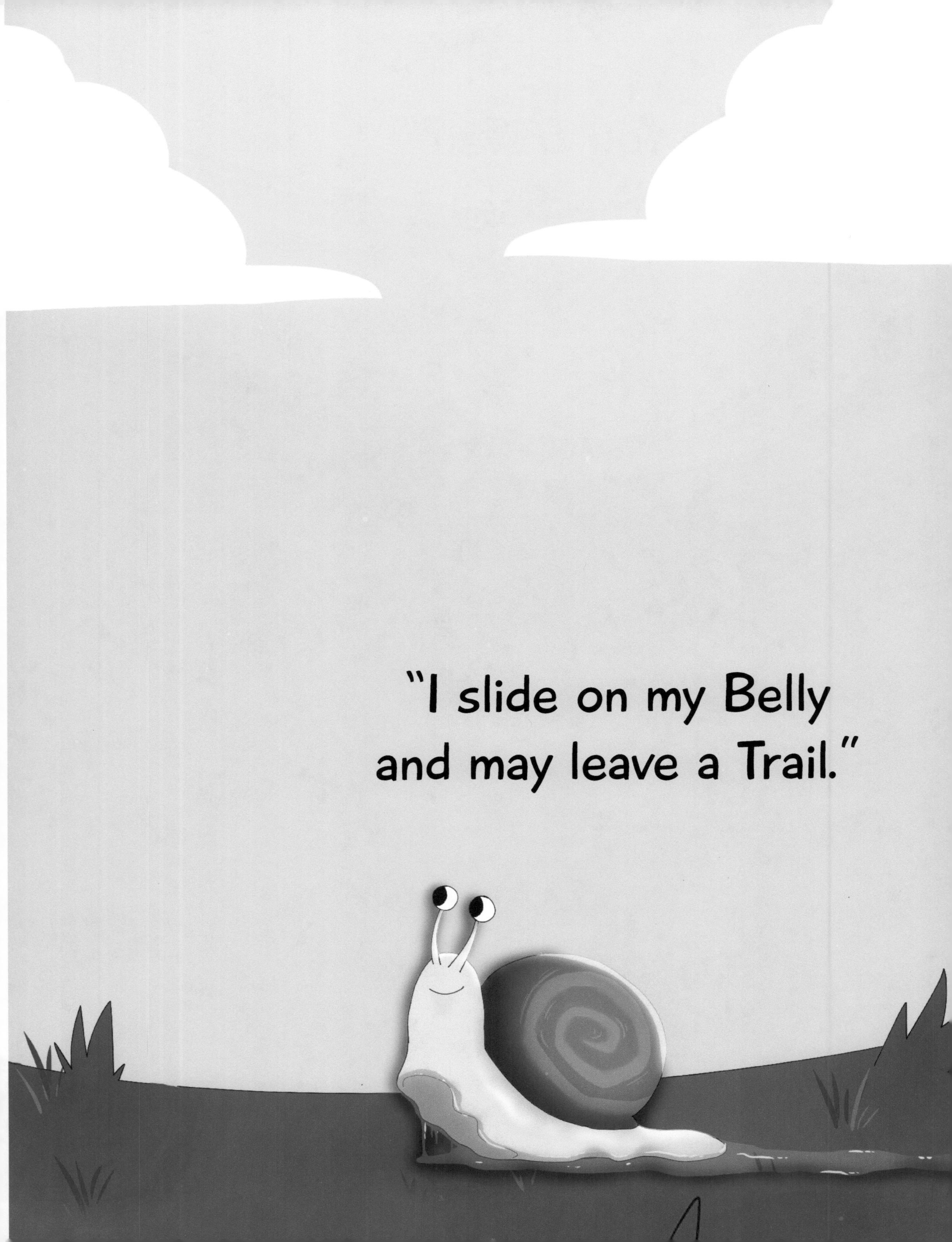

"I slide on my Belly
and may leave a Trail."

"How Do You Travel?"
I said to the whale.

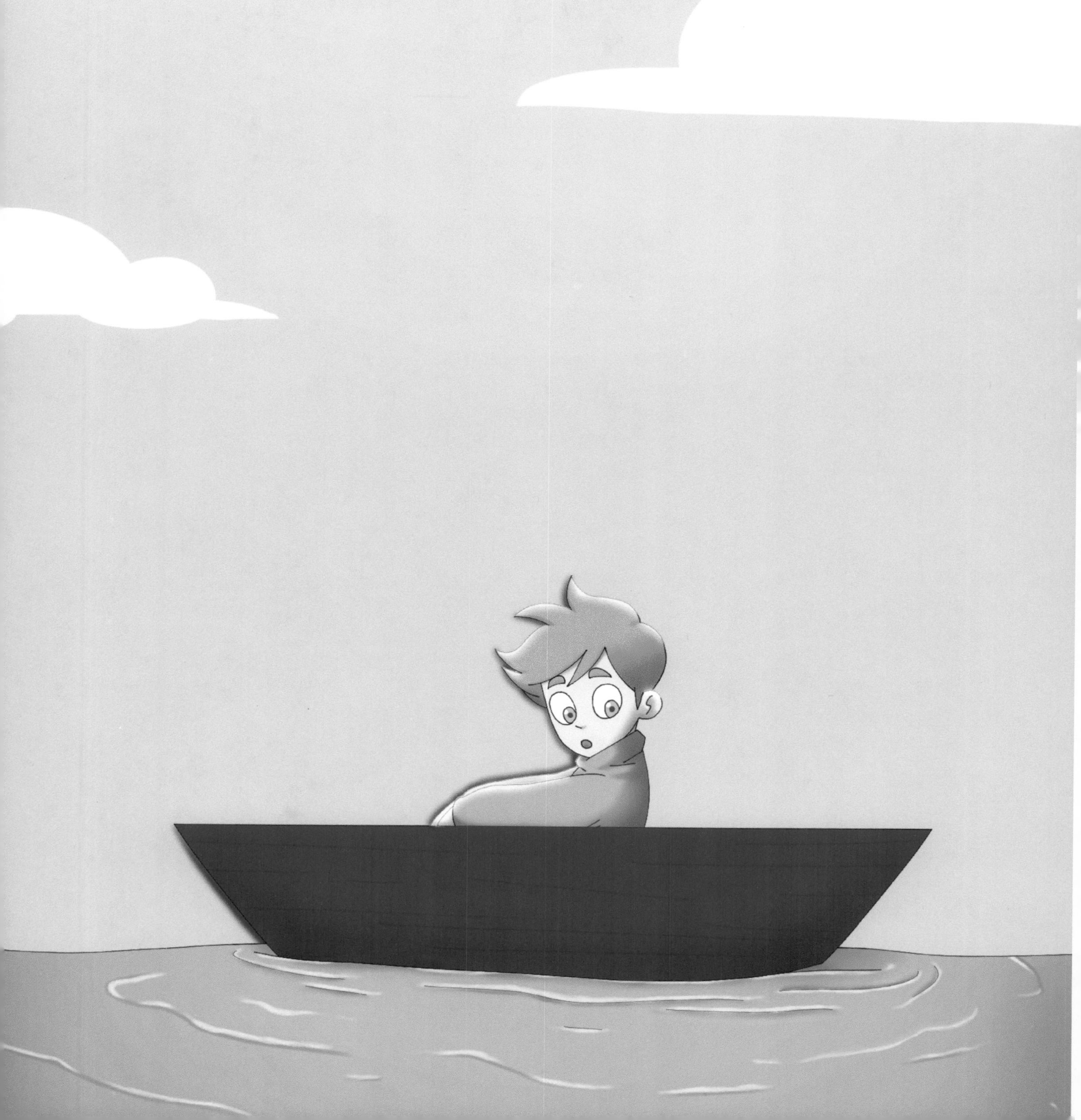

"I cruise through the ocean,
fluttering my tail."

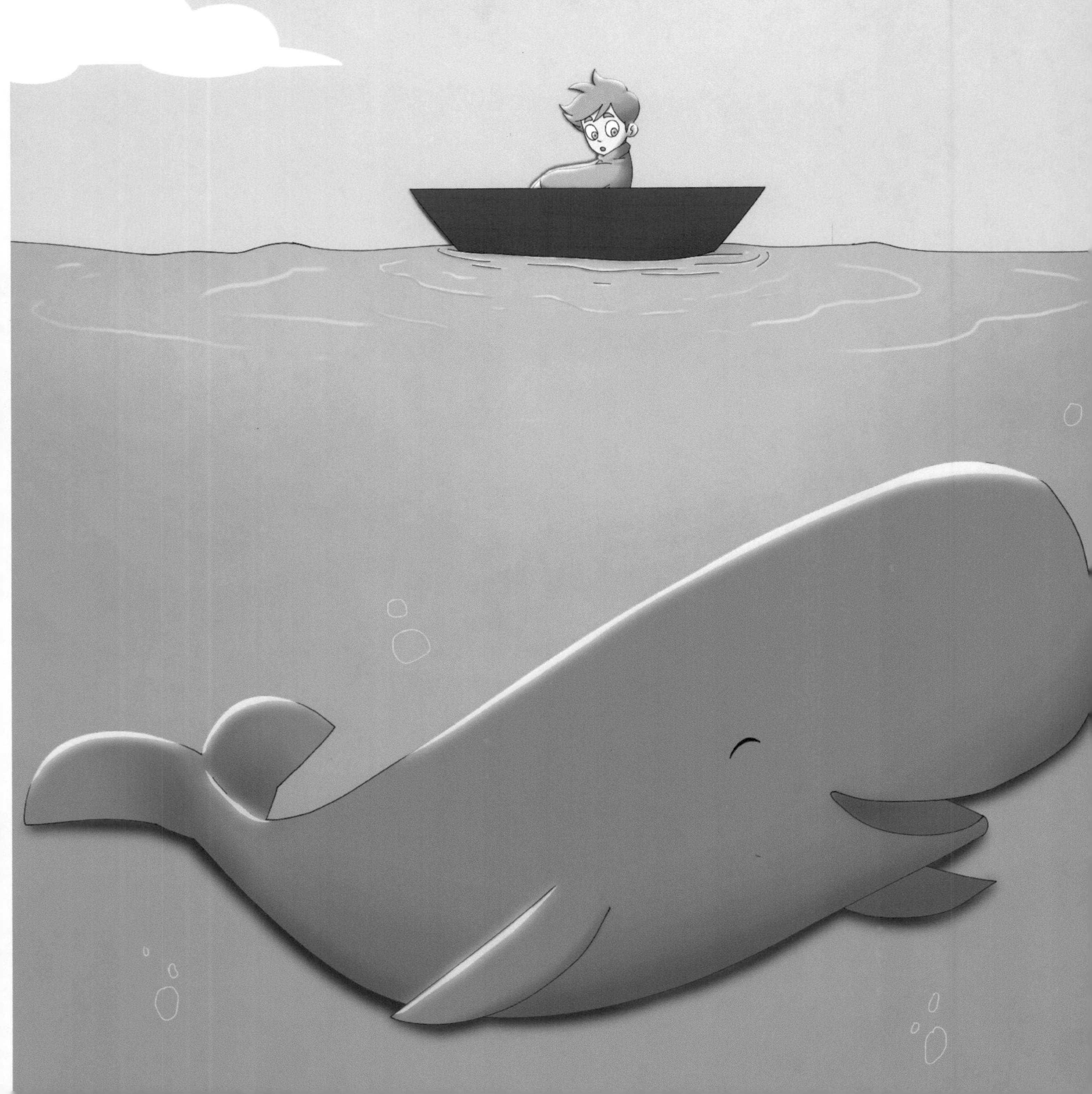

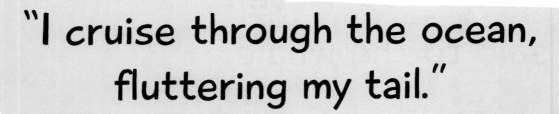

"How Do You Travel?"
I said to the Boy.

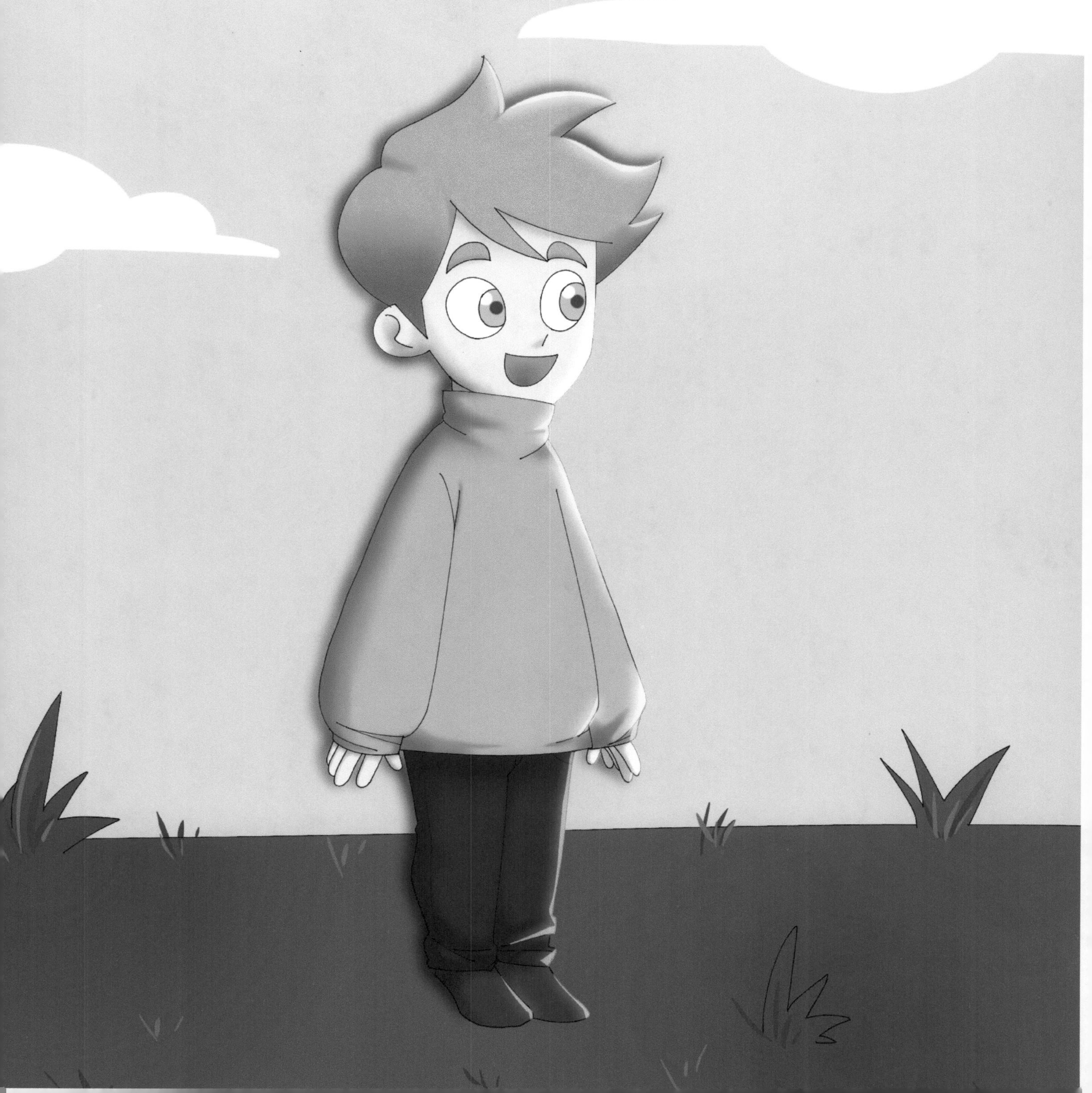

"I go many ways!"
He said with such joy.

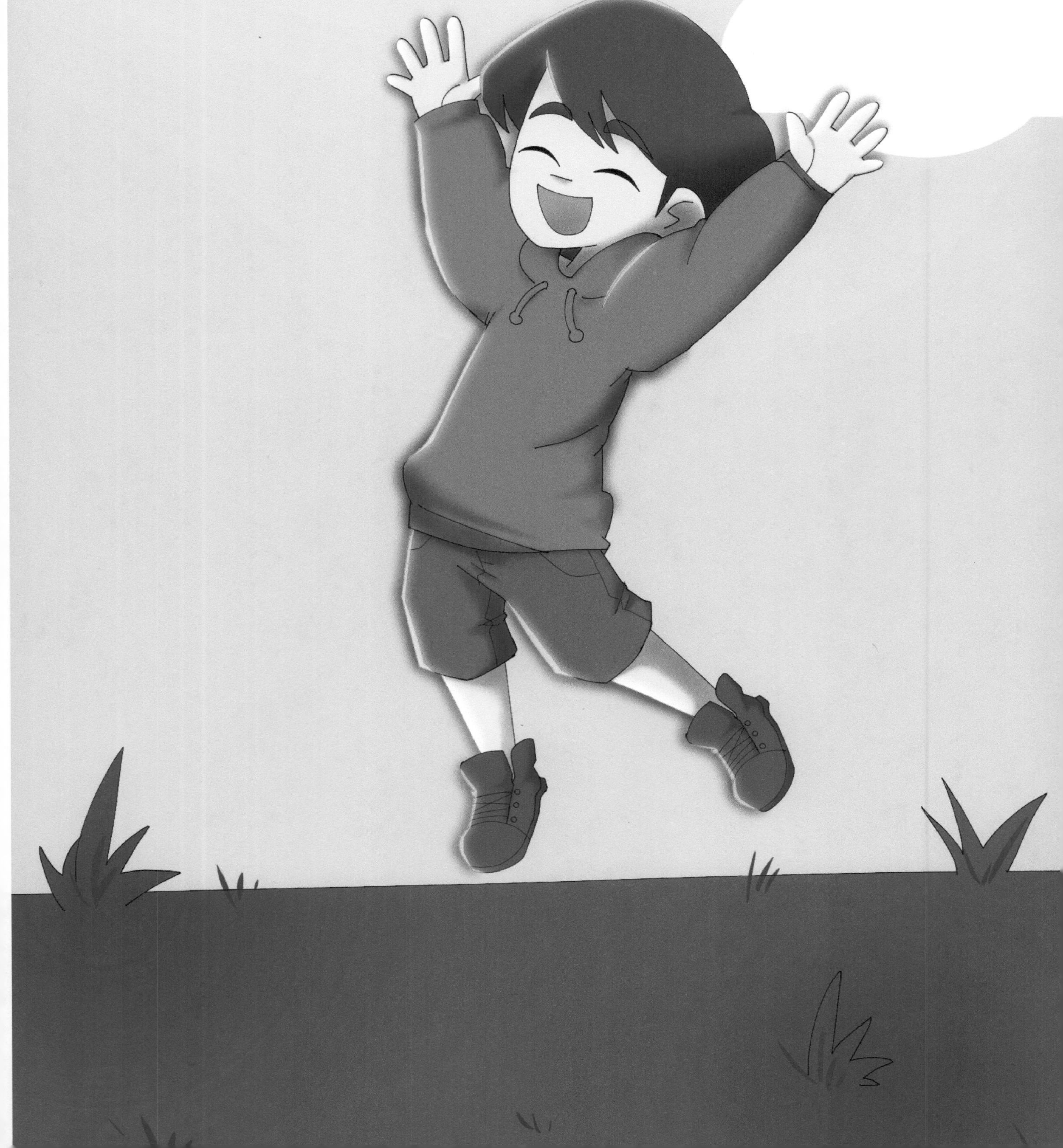

I can walk,

I can run,

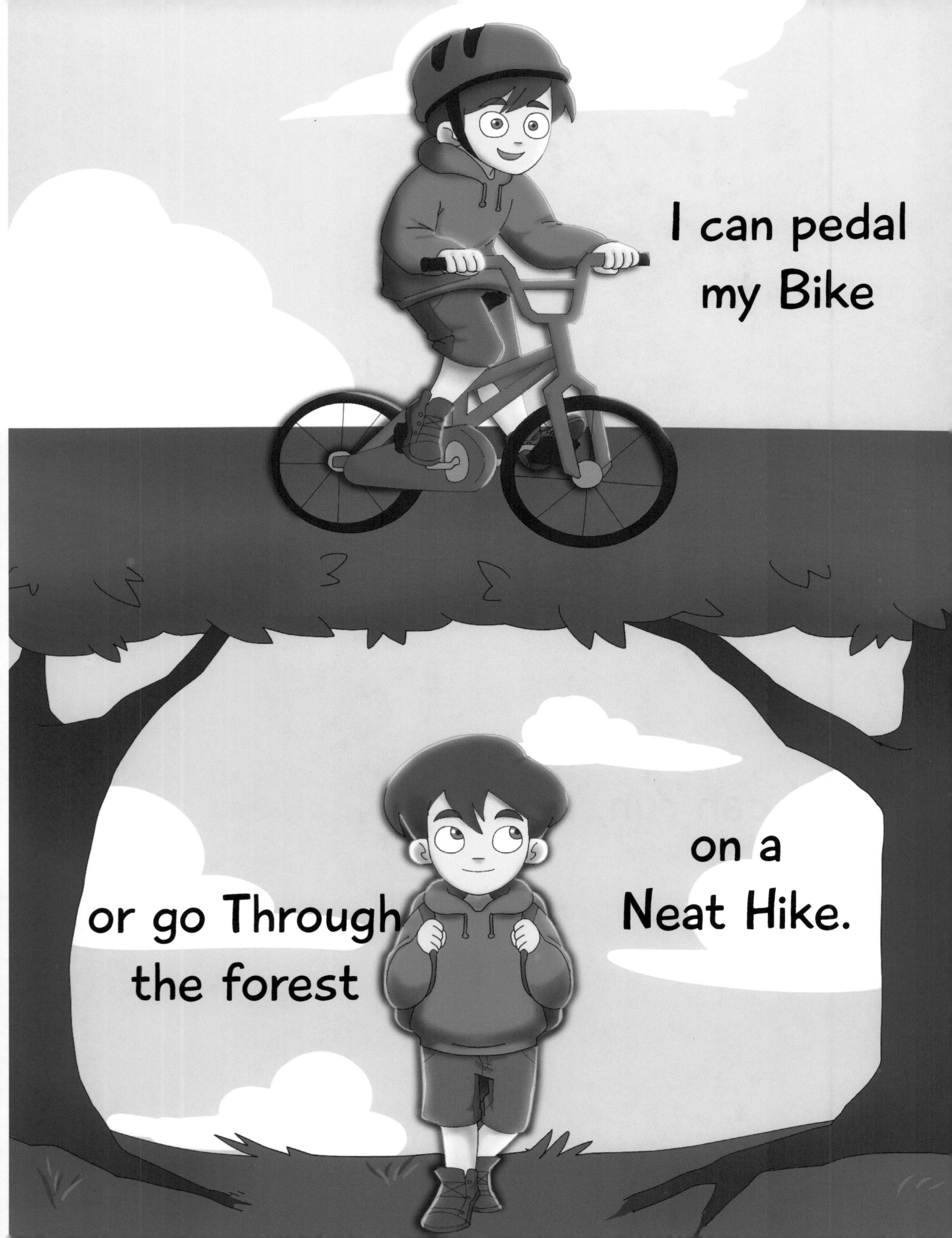

I can pedal
my Bike

or go Through
the forest

on a
Neat Hike.

I can skip,

I can skateboard,
or ride in a car

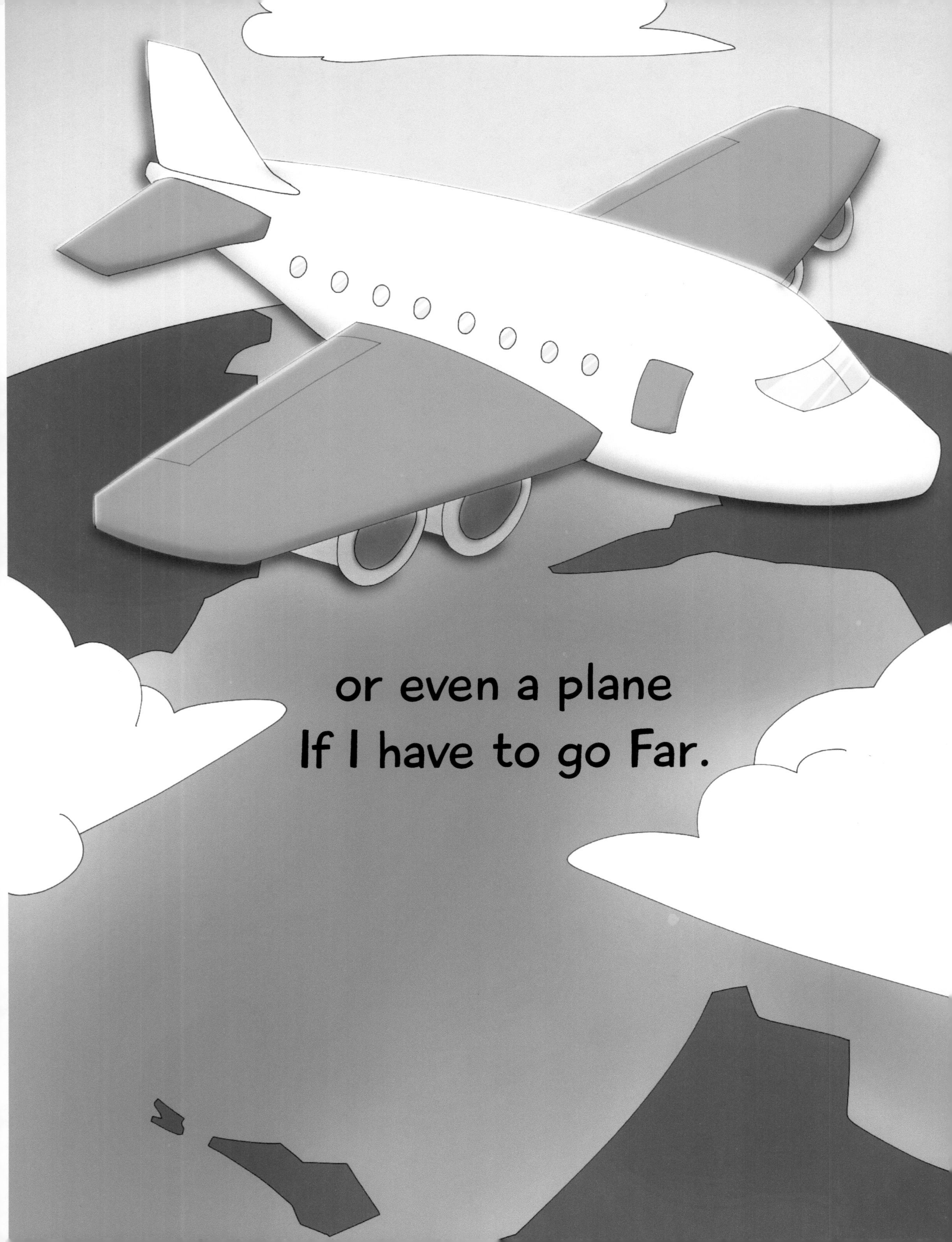

or even a plane
If I have to go Far.

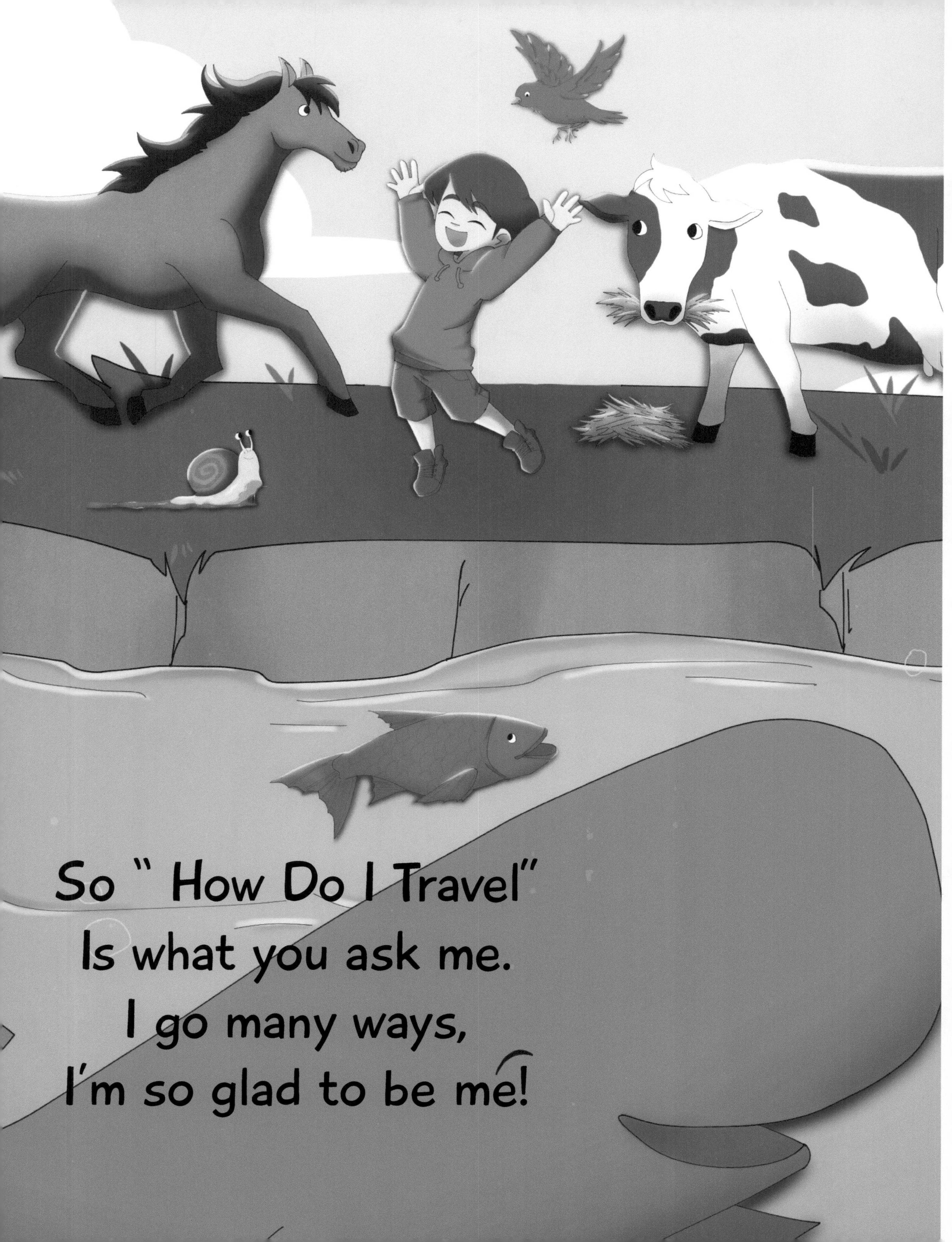

So " How Do I Travel"
Is what you ask me.
I go many ways,
I'm so glad to be me!

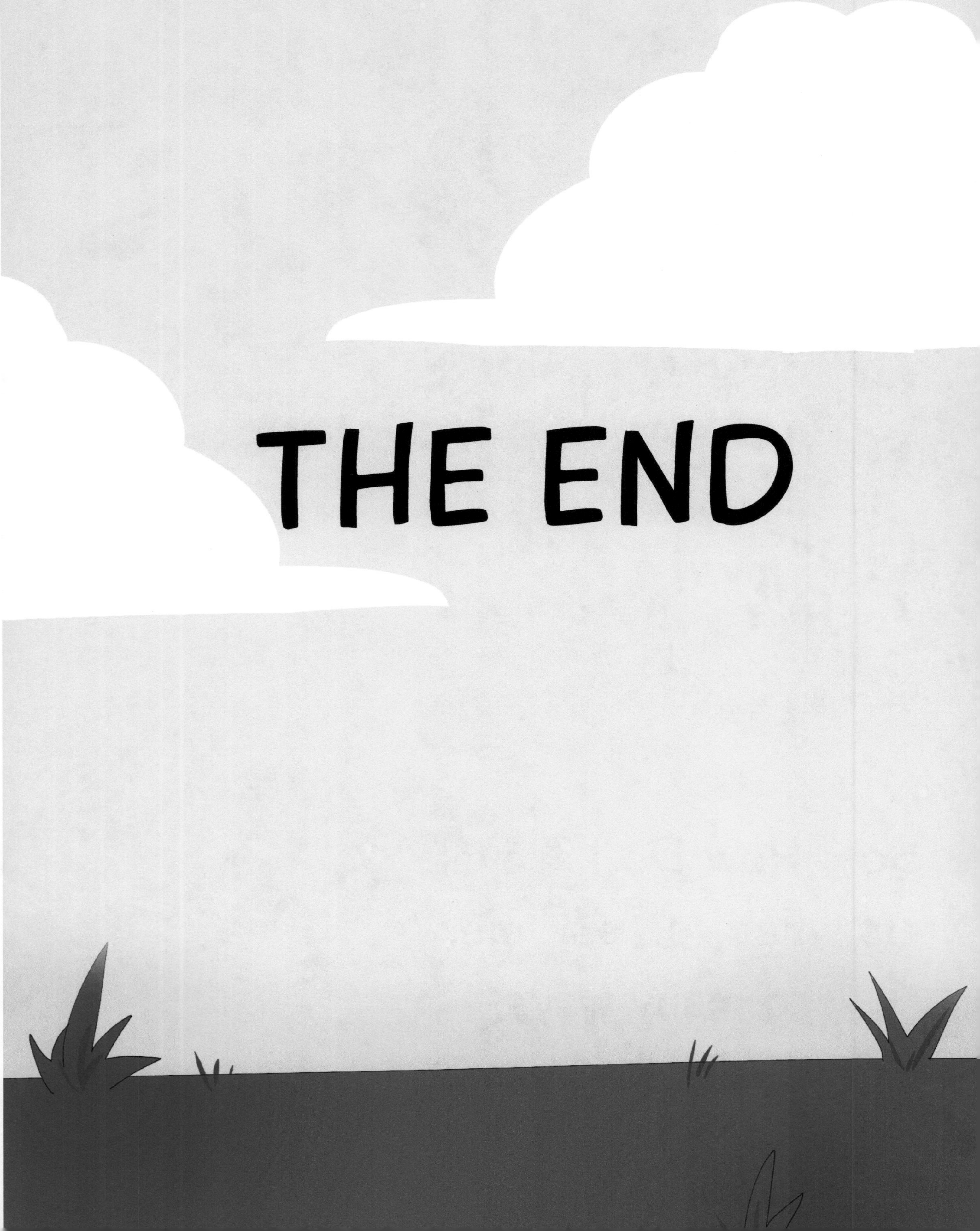
THE END

CPSIA information can be obtained
at www.ICGtesting.com
Printed in the USA
BVHW022014221122
652525BV00009B/737

To:

Wylie Jane

READ, READ, READ!!!

Love,
Kathleen Joy Campion